AMERIGO VESPUCCI

ALSO BY RONALD SYME

AMERIGO VESPUCCI
SCIENTIST AND SAILOR

RONALD SYME
illustrated by WILLIAM STOBBS

William Morrow & Company New York

When Amerigo Vespucci was a boy, Florence was a lovely and interesting city in which to live. The narrow, winding streets were lined with elegant, red-tiled houses. Here and there handsome archways led to the splendid mansions of the nobility.

Men and women of all classes thronged the pavements: prosperous merchants in sober but expensive attire, brightly dressed young aristocrats, students, painters, and sculptors. Horse-drawn, curtained carriages containing the wives and daughters of the city's wealthiest families clattered along the cobbled streets. Throughout the long summers, the Italian sky was a warm and cloudless blue.

Beginning in the middle of the fourteenth century Florence had become in one hundred years the wealthiest and finest city in Italy. It had surpassed its ancient rival, Venice. Even the great port of Genoa, rising on rocky hillsides from the sea, could not compare with it in the splendor of its buildings or the wealth of its stately banking houses. Sprawling across the great highways that ran north and south, surrounded by the richest agricultural valleys in all Italy, Florence was supreme.

When their son Amerigo was born in 1454, the family was already one of the most distinguished in the city. Their wealth was solidly founded on the gold coinage, good throughout Europe, which lay in the coffers of their trading and banking offices. The produce of their prosperous country estates, situated a few miles outside Florence, increased their wealth. Nastagio Vespucci, Amerigo's father, was the city's outstanding political leader. But, being a shrewd, cultured, and careful man, he had no intention of allowing his four sons to enjoy in idle leisure the endless amusements that abounded for the young people of Florence.

Amerigo's two elder brothers, Antonio and Girolamo, were sent to the great University of Pisa to complete their education. Bernardo, his younger brother, followed them a few years later.

Amerigo was the one chosen by his father to enter the family business, when he was eighteen years old. Strange to say, although he didn't go to the university, he was better educated than his brothers.

Giorgio Antonio Vespucci, Amerigo's uncle, had given him his education. He was dean of the cathedral, an expert on art, a great thinker, and an authority on geography. The system of education at the universities of those days was formal and traditional. White-haired and scholarly Fra Giorgio had progressive views of his own.

He taught Amerigo mathematics and flawless Latin. He instructed the young man in writing clearly, concisely, and fluently in his native Italian language. In the quiet surroundings of his private library, he unrolled maps and placed them on the table for young Amerigo to study.

Wonderful maps they were of far lands still wrapped in mystery. Asia was known to exist many thousands of miles away to the east, but knowledge about it was vague. Somewhere between the Red Sea and China lay India. The southern coasts of Africa had yet to be explored. The entire New World, the whole American continent, was undreamed of. Not

even Fra Giorgio was able to predict its existence.

"The theory that the world is round is generally accepted by educated men of today," he told Amerigo one day, when they were looking at maps together. "The idea was first suggested by Pythagoras, the Greek philosopher, nearly two thousand years ago. Aristotle, the most famous of all Greek philosophers, gave his support to the theory. Ptolemy, the Egyptian, based his map of the world on that belief. His map, which we still use today, was drawn thirteen hundred years ago. If the world *is* round, then it might actually be possible to reach India by sailing westward across the Atlantic Ocean. That is, of course, if some daring navigator and crew were prepared to take a ship on such a long and dangerous voyage."

Vespucci studied the Ptolemy map. The suggestion that his uncle had made was startling. According to Ptolemy, the most easterly place

10

PTOLEMY MAP

in Asia was named Cattigara. If a ship sailed
in a westward direction from it, the vessel
would enter the seas that washed the tropical
shores of India.

"The master of that vessel would have to
exert great care not to go too far south," suggested Vespucci. "If he did so, he would find
himself near the equator where, I have read, all
life becomes impossible due to the intense
heat."

11

His uncle nodded.

"One certainly reads that, my son," he agreed. "But I myself hesitate to accept the statement." Fra Giorgio told Vespucci how King Necho of Egypt a long time before had sent a Phoenician ship on a voyage around Africa, and that Hanno, of the great city of Carthage, was said to have sailed from Spain on a voyage that took him past the southern tip of Africa and into the Red Sea. At least two other navigators were supposed to have accomplished similar voyages.

"Now, unless the fragmentary reports we have of those voyages are all false," he went on, "one or more ships have crossed the equator, and yet the crews survived. It is all very puzzling. I fear that the answers will not be forthcoming in my lifetime."

At twenty-one, Amerigo Vespucci, now a merchant-trader, had become a handsome, sharp-featured young man with an aquiline

nose, a heavy chin, and wide, observant eyes. He was of medium height and sturdy build.

Few of his friends or clients were aware of his continuing study of geography, an unusual interest for a man of business. Still fascinated by the endless riddles that confronted geographers, map makers, and learned men everywhere, he acquired some familiarity with astronomy and enlarged his knowledge of Europe on several business trips to France and Spain. Other merchants regarded him as an honest and agreeable young man, who was popular on account of his generous nature and amusing conversation. Whenever he returned from trips to foreign countries, he brought with him numerous presents for his friends and their children.

Vespucci's pleasant way of life continued until he was twenty-three years old. At that time Florence was defeated in a conflict with neighboring Italian states. The city was impoverished, and wealthy citizens were compelled to pay heavy taxes. Business became difficult and profits smaller.

Vespucci continued to trade in a great variety of goods, ranging from dried fish and poultry to carpets, wine, and spices brought overland from India, but the great wealth of the family was heavily reduced. His father died in 1482, and the loss of his experience and of his valuable personal contacts in all

the cities along the Mediterranean was a further heavy blow to the family enterprises.

Amerigo's brothers went into business on their own account, but none of them prospered. On more than one occasion, Vespucci had to find large sums of money to pay their debts and even, at times, to support their families. He was so busy tending to Vespucci family affairs that he was forced to neglect his private life, and he did not marry.

The great Medici family lived in Florence, although their enormous wealth was spread all over Europe. They, too, owned trading and banking houses, but the hard times that had come to the city had left unharmed their wealth in other countries. In 1483, the two heirs of this great fortune were Lorenzo de' Medici, age twenty, and Giovanni, age seventeen. They were pleasant young men but unskilled in business. Fortunately, they were smart enough to realize that they were incapable of supervising their family's interests.

"Come and manage our business," they invited Vespucci. "Your family and ours have always been friends. You have the experience we lack, so we will not interfere in your direction of our business affairs."

Vespucci accepted the offer. The Medici brothers treated him generously. They regarded him as a personal friend, went for long country rides with him, and insisted that he attend magnificent receptions at the Medici palace.

Being reasonably wealthy again, Vespucci was able to spend more time brooding over his maps. The knowledge of geographers had increased very little during the past thousand years. Even the most expensive charts he could buy taught him almost nothing beyond what he had learned from his uncle. The one area that was an exception was the west coast of Africa. Intrepid Portuguese sea-

men were steadily pushing farther south in their explorations there.

The recent invention of printing, however, was spreading new ideas. Curiosity about the entire world was being stimulated. Navigators, cartographers (map makers), and university professors were beginning to wonder about the Western (Atlantic) Ocean, which was still often referred to as the unknown Sea of Darkness. The age was a fascinating and exciting one in which to live. Dividing his time between maps and science, and mustard, silks, and cutlery, Vespucci had a busy life.

In 1488, when Vespucci was thirty-four years old, the exciting news reached Europe that Bartholomeu Dias, the Portuguese seaman, had actually reached the southern end of Africa. The first of a brilliant series of geographical discoveries had been made. Perhaps Vespucci sensed that an age of discovery, which was to create enormous wealth for Spain and Portugal, was about to begin. He wrote to Lorenzo de' Medici:

> I think it necessary that I should remain in Spain to supervise our business interests there. Many profitable enterprises could be undertaken in that country and there is an increasing demand for the goods and services which we can supply.

Lorenzo agreed, and early in 1492 Amerigo Vespucci, the Florentine merchant, opened an office in the southern Spanish city of Seville. This great city, lying some seventy miles inland from the sea, was built on the banks of the wide and deep Guadalquivir River and had become a flourishing port.

Vespucci's interest in maps and the sea was freshly stirred in the bustling town. Men were still talking about that odd Italian fellow, Cristobal Colon, or Cristoforo Colombo, who had recently sailed off on a frightening voyage across the Sea of Darkness. No doubt he was dead by this time. How could any man hope to survive such an impossible journey? To reach India by sailing westward would necessitate an almost endless voyage across unknown oceans haunted by strange monsters, vast whirlpools, and possibly demons in human disguise.

These common fears of the day did not lessen Vespucci's interest in exploration. He enjoyed strolling along the busy river wharves to gaze at seaworn little ships and their bronzed crews handling the cargoes they had brought from Africa and Britain and Egypt. Leaning on a ponderous mooring post, Vespucci allowed his imagination to stray down the river and out to the seas far beyond the coast of Spain. Were Columbus and the men with him really dead? Were they even now making some discovery that would astonish the world?

The answer arrived in Seville a year after Vespucci had set up his office there. The date was March, 1493.

"The great Colon has returned." Vespucci heard the event being discussed on the wharves. "He has found land across the sea! He reached India by sailing westward. It is said that the coast he discovered has great wealth in gold and pearls. It is not as far to that country as we all believed."

The news astonished Vespucci. His uncle had taught him that the circumference of the earth at the equator was nearly 26,000 miles. Other wise men agreed with that figure. But Columbus had apparently reached India after a westward voyage of some 3,000 miles. Either India—or was it some part of China—extended much farther eastward than any geographer believed, or the circumference of the world had been estimated incorrectly. Vespucci felt disappointed. He suspected that there was some error in the conclusions of Columbus. Without having more information, though, he could not discover what it was.

One result of this first voyage was very clear: Columbus's discovery had started a first-class dispute between the rival countries of Portugal and Spain. Portuguese seamen had come to regard the Atlantic Ocean almost as their private property. National jealousy made them insist that they were legally entitled to a share of any territories discovered along its western limits.

When the two countries had reached the point of going to war, the Pope was asked to settle the dispute. By the Treaty of Tordesillas in 1494, it was decreed that for a distance of 370 leagues (approximately 1500 miles) westward from the Cape Verde Islands off West Africa, the ocean should be regarded as belonging to Portugal. Everything west of that point should belong to Spain. Neither the Pope nor anyone else was aware then that it passed closed to the mouth of the Amazon River and thence southward through a large section of the tropical country that came later to be called Brazil.

Columbus, fitting the discoveries he had made into the theories about geography that were generally held in his day, concluded that the land he had discovered on the western side of the Atlantic must be India. The legendary city of Cattigara depicted by Ptolemy probably lay somewhere to the south of the route he had followed. As his voyage had been much shorter than expected, earlier theories as to the probable circumference of the earth, he declared, must be wrong.

I see that the world is not so large as the people say it is. One degree on the equator is fifty-six and two-third miles. . . . This is a fact and whatever anyone says to the contrary is only words.

This statement sounded strange to Vespucci. He had been taught, and calculated for himself, that a degree was sixty-six and one third miles. (The correct figure is actually 69.172 miles.) Because of the variation in these figures, by the time Columbus set off on his second voyage of discovery in September, 1493, Vespucci had begun to doubt that the newly discovered land was India.

The Medici business interests in Spain flourished and grew under Vespucci's capable and honest administration. He had developed a firm friendship with Giannetto Berardi, a Florentine like himself. Berardi was responsible to the Spanish government for equipping ships with the stores necessary for long voyages overseas. Vespucci was supplying many of the items used. He did so in such an efficient manner that Berardi fully trusted him.

In December, 1495, while Columbus was still in the West Indies, Berardi died. In his will he named Vespucci to help take care of his business affairs. The Spanish government promptly gave Vespucci a commission to handle the supplies and stores for several ships, a contract on which Berardi had been working at the time of his death.

While Vespucci was filling this contract, word came from Columbus that he had reached land on the western side of the Atlantic at a point some ten degrees north of the equator. After spending some time in that area, he had again sailed north to Hispaniola, where he had left a number of his men during his first voyage.

Why North? Vespucci asked himself. According to the various maps of the world, Cattigara was situated about eight and a half degrees south of the equator. Columbus made his landfall at ten degrees *north*. Surely he

should have turned southward in order to reach that cape. Was the admiral himself beginning to have doubts as to whether this land he had discovered was indeed India? Was he bent on searching for some other passage that would take him farther west?

Vespucci went on poring over his collection of maps and charts, on which he had already filled in the latest territories discovered by Columbus. Nothing the admiral said seemed to agree with previous theories. Was Cuba, which Columbus believed was not an island but the mainland, really the same as Kubla, the great Chinese empire of Kubla Khan? This empire had been described more than 170 years ago by the Venetian overland explorer, Marco Polo.

The whole fascinating problem was having a tremendous influence on Vespucci. Unknown to himself, his nature was changing. While he continued to deal by day with shipments of olive oil, and currants, and cotton from Egypt, his nights were spent in eager geographical study. About this time he recalled his former interest in astronomy. Equipped with the best telescope he could buy, he began to study the stars. Meanwhile, Columbus did not push his explorations south of the equator. To Amerigo Vespucci, the knowledgeable amateur geographer, the admiral's delay was puzzling.

The third voyage of Columbus in 1498 was regarded by many of the learned men of Europe with considerable apathy and scorn. They had realized what Vespucci was quick to perceive. Too many discrepancies appeared between what the admiral said and what common-sense observers with him saw for themselves. The natives he had brought home in his ships were certainly not the Indians of India. Nor were they Chinese. Where were the great palaces and temples reported by European travelers who had followed the overland caravan routes from Arabia to India? Where *was* the empire of Kubla Khan? What could have happened to Cattigara? Was Columbus correct in claiming that the world was much smaller than anyone else supposed?

Mariners at that time knew how to ascertain their latitude, that is, their distance north or south of the equator, with reasonable accuracy. It was found by a simple measurement of the altitude of the polestar above the horizon. But longitude, or the distance east or west, could only be accurately found if one knew the correct time.

The meridian through Greenwich, in England, was accepted as zero degree longitude, and distances east or west were measured from that line.

When mariners began to venture out on the vastness of the Atlantic Ocean, they had no means of keeping track of the time with accuracy; that is the time in the port from which they had sailed. The clocks of that period did not operate well on board ship as the violent motion of the vessel upset the delicate adjustment of the mechanism. Similarly, an hourglass was not accurate because the ship's motion caused the sand to run out too fast. Sometimes a sleepy ship's boy, assigned to the duty of watching the hourglass, failed to turn it punctually.

Without an accurate means of timekeeping early seamen had to rely on their judgment of the length of each day's run by their ships. After several weeks at sea, errors usually caused them to believe that the vessel was either farther east or farther west than it really was.

Vespucci began to work on this problem of determining the longitude. His theory was that it might be possible to estimate longi-

34

tude exactly by making certain lunar measurements. The moon is relatively swift
moving. The planets are slow moving. By
ascertaining the speed with which the moon
passed a chosen planet, he might obtain use-
ful data. The first experiments he made were
with the planet Mars. L 1485654

As he became more involved in the project,
he decided to make a journey of exploration
himself in order to put his theory to the test.

The Medici brothers granted him permission to take the trip. They realized that if Vespucci made some worthwhile discovery, he would be very popular with King Ferdinand and Queen Isabella of Spain. Royal favor would undoubtedly increase the profitable business being done by the Medici firm in Seville.

Vespucci found little difficulty in carrying out his plan. He was forty-five years old and of excellent repute. Through his business in Seville he was already familiar with ships and numerous sea captains. The Spanish Admiralty had great faith in him. His knowledge of mathematics, astronomy, and geography astonished those to whom he displayed it. The Medici family were prepared to make an investment in the proposed voyage.

Vespucci sailed with a squadron of six ships in May, 1499. The expedition was officially under the supreme command of

Alonso de Ojeda, a wealthy favorite of the royal court. He was not a seaman nor did he understand navigation; he merely acted as the representative of King Ferdinand and Queen Isabella, the strict and capable rulers of Spain.

A professional seaman named Juan de la Cosa, who had accompanied Columbus across the Atlantic on his first and second voyages, acted as chief pilot for Ojeda's squadron. Vespucci's duties were to serve as astronomer and cartographer. He also represented the interests of the wealthy merchants who had invested sums of money in the expedition.

The ships were typical of the period, being three-masted and extremely high at bow and stern. By modern standards they were absurdly small, for the largest was not more than 170 tons. Spain owned much larger vessels, but they were unpopular with veteran seamen on the Atlantic. When a deep ocean swell rose under the middle of their length, they were inclined to "hog," or bend downward at bow and stern. This movement often preceded the vessel's breaking in half.

After taking on fresh water, firewood, and food at the Canary Islands off the coast of Morocco, the vessels swung their ponderous bows westward across the Atlantic. Twenty-four days later they sighted land north of the Amazon River. Vespucci wrote:

> Seeing land we gave thanks to God. We put out our boats with about six men each and pulled toward the shore. We found the land heavily covered with trees which were most amazing not only in height but in their greenness, since they are never denuded of all their leaves. They had a fragrant smell, being all aromatic, and gave forth such refreshing odors that we were greatly invigorated.

They were the first Europeans to reach the

American coast so far south. Ojeda, like most Spanish explorers, was more interested in acquiring wealth for himself than in mapping unknown coasts. Hurriedly he sailed off north with four ships. He was bound for what Columbus had named the Coast of Pearls, the mainland opposite Trinidad. Juan de la Cosa went with him. Vespucci was left with two ships to go exploring on his own.

Ptolemy's city of Cattigara was supposed to lie eight and a half degrees south of the equator. But Vespucci, now in four degrees north latitude, was puzzled by the fact that the coastline stretched south of him in an apparently unending line. There was no sign of its yielding to the open seaway that was supposed to lead to India.

Vespucci ordered his two ships to sail south. While cruising off the coast, his crew discovered to their surprise that the sea was no longer salt. It had become fresh enough to drink. On that same day they sighted the 150-mile wide mouth of the Amazon River.

With his astrolabe, the instrument used to observe the positions of heavenly bodies, Vespucci calculated that he was now four degrees south of the equator. New and unknown stars were swinging across the night sky, and he was busy placing them on his chart of the heavens.

Huddled in a thick coat as protection against the heavy tropical dew, he spent entire nights on the lonely deck, where the unending creak of the rigging and the wash of the dark sea against the tarred hull were the only sounds that disturbed the deep stillness.

A thousand miles down the coast from the point where he had first sighted Brazil, the South Equatorial Current, sweeping up to the equator, defied his ships any further progress. He wrote:

It ran from southeast to northwest and was so great and ran so furiously that we were terribly frightened and hastened away out of this great danger. . . . We decided to point our bows to the northwest and sail to northern parts.

Vespucci gave that order with a feeling of bitter disappointment. He believed that, had he managed to go a little farther south, he might have come in time to Cattigara and the open sea that would lead to India. He modestly refrained from taking pride in the knowledge that he was the first European to sail south of the equator on the westward side of the Atlantic. He also already had mapped a thousand miles of unknown coast and much of the southern skies.

His two ships reached Trinidad in August. Vespucci anchored at a careful distance of one mile from the coast of the island, known to be inhabited by a race of ferocious canni-

bals named the Caribs. He ordered his men
to arm themselves. Then, with twenty-two
companions, he was rowed ashore.

The sight of these strange beings stepping
onto the white beach was too much for the
Caribs. The great crowd of them who had
been lining the shore retreated hurriedly into
the twilit depths of the vast tropical forest.

Vespucci set an example that later explorers would have done well to follow. He

45

smiled and made friendly gestures to the dim figures among the trees, holding out presents of mirrors, small knives, and fish-hooks. Gradually the Caribs, still carrying their bows and arrows, gathered around him and began to take the gifts he offered. Later that morning Vespucci and his followers marched six miles inland to a village where they were given a meal of fish, fruit, and a kind of bread. During this meal, the explorer, who must have had a strong stomach, diligently questioned the Caribs as to their cannibal habits and examined a number of human bones and skulls. Toward the early afternoon he marched back with his men to the beach, still on the best of terms with the vast crowd of naked warriors by whom the Europeans were surrounded.

Not caring to delay, we departed with many parrots of various colors and with friendly good feeling.

46

When his two ships left Trinidad, Vespucci steered westward along the coast of what is now Venezuela and Colombia, then still un-explored. He and his men were the first Europeans that the Indians of those countries had seen. Columbus had sighted Venezuela a year earlier, but he had not investigated it fully.

In the great stern cabin under the poop of his vessel, Vespucci was busy drawing charts

47

of this coast. All the time he kept in his mind the problem of how mariners could determine longitude. During those nights spent on the South American coast in August, 1499, Vespucci tested his own method of measuring the speed with which the moon passed the planet Mars. The idea was extremely involved. He realized that before master mariners could use it, tables of the positions and movements of the moon and a number of planets would have to be prepared. The necessary data could only be gathered through many observations at different points on the world's surface. But the fact remained that after more nights of practical astronomy on the deck of his ship, Vespucci was able to come up with a reasonably accurate computation of his longitude. He had hit on a method that would be used by sea captains for the next 250 years, until accurate time-keeping chronometers were invented.

The Indians of the country that Vespucci christened "Veneçuela," or Little Venice, were a naturally fierce people. Every time the seamen landed to replenish their ships with water and firewood, they were forced to fight on the beaches.

Firearms were still too primitive to be of any real use. The battles were waged with swords and crossbows against thrown javelins, wooden spears, and arrows. Two of the sailors were killed and many others wounded.

One such fight occurred near La Guaira, where a strong party of seamen rowed ashore. Confronted by a cliff some 200 feet high, they found a beaten-earth path that led up its face. On reaching the scrub-covered plateau at the top of this cliff, they were suddenly attacked on three sides by several hundred Indians.

Luckily for Vespucci and his men they were wearing armor. The steel deflected the

well-aimed arrows and lessened the crushing impact of heavy blows from stone-headed clubs. But such was the intense heat that the sailors, sweating under the weight of their steel breastplates and helmets, were soon staggering and exhausted.

One hundred and fifty Indians were killed on that sun-scorched plateau and the remainder fled. Vespucci led his men into the adjacent village, where they drank all the water they could find, set fire to the thatched huts, and retreated hurriedly to the beach. They spent the next three weeks aboard their anchored ships, recovering from the wounds they had suffered.

September came when Vespucci was still at Cape de la Vela, some 500 miles east of Panama. He had explored a total of three thousand miles of coast since he set off on his own. Now he must hurry home. The *teredos,* marine borer worms, had riddled the underwater hulls of his vessels. The crew were grumbling at the almost incessant pumping they had to perform to keep the ships afloat.

On September 19, he left the coast of Colombia and sailed north to Hispaniola. Leaving Ojeda and the pilot la Cosa there with their four ships, Vespucci set sail for Spain, passing through the Bahamas on the way.

The voyage was a terrible one. The ships were sea weary and leaked incessantly. Food supplies in strife-torn Hispaniola, where the quarrelsome Spaniards were at one another's throats, were almost unobtainable. The sails were rotten from constant soaking with tropical dew and drying in hot sunshine. Thus, it was not until June, 1500, that Vespucci navigated his own two ships safely back to Cadiz.

On reaching Seville, he wrote a long and fascinating letter to his friend and patron, Lorenzo de' Medici, in which he gave a full account of everything he had seen and done. Vespucci made no false claims nor did he exaggerate in any way. The letter was concise, careful, and vivid, one that was worthy of a man whose reputation for integrity and intelligence was well known.

Interesting news awaited Vespucci in Spain. While he had been on the coast of Venezuela, Vasco da Gama, the Portuguese seaman, had rounded the Cape of Good Hope, reached India, and returned safely to Lisbon. A sea road to India had been found at last.

King Ferdinand and Queen Isabella were delighted with the results of Vespucci's voyage. He had explored and mapped a great deal of territory that undoubtedly belonged to Spain. He had proved himself a careful and competent explorer and navigator. His lunar measurements of longitude were too difficult for most people to understand, but it did seem that Vespucci had a much more accurate idea of the distances he had sailed than all previous explorers. Almost at once their majesties promised him three ships in which to set off on a second voyage of discovery. This time the royal treasury would meet the cost of fitting out the vessels.

While geographers were beginning to regard Ptolemy's ancient map with more and more distrust, a Spanish explorer named Vicente Pinzon returned home in July, 1500. He reported having reached the coast of Brazil ten degrees south of the equator. From that point he had sailed north to the most easterly elbow of the coast. He had not sighted anything that resembled Cattigara. The map was thus finally proved inaccurate. Further proof of this startling new fact was the news that had reached Lisbon in May, 1500. Pedro Cabral, a Portuguese explorer, reached the coast of Brazil in a latitude eighteen degrees south of the equator and

thence sailed northward for some distance. He, too, had sighted no westward passage.

Poring over his newly drawn maps and checking over the distances he had sailed, another thought came to Vespucci. Much of Brazil undoubtedly lay east of the Line of Demarcation. Thus it legally belonged to Portugal. He could scarcely go exploring it in Spanish ships without incurring the anger and jealousy of the Portuguese.

Vespucci honorably dropped his idea of a fresh voyage on behalf of Spain. He explained his reasons to Ferdinand and Isabella. When they released him from his undertaking, he approached King Emanuel of Portugal.

That monarch was already well aware of Vespucci's important achievements on his recent voyage. He wasted no time in placing three ships at his disposal.

Amerigo Vespucci sailed out of Lisbon's

mud-banked Tagus River on May 13, 1501.

He was glad to be on the open seas again. By this time the fascination of unknown waters and strange coasts had thoroughly gripped him. The whole great puzzle of this New World was entrancing. Was it really the eastern coast of Asia? Or was it—could it possibly be—some entirely new continent? This idea was undoubtedly already passing through Vespucci's mind. Before he made any public reference to it, he had to be sure of his facts. He might be able to prove the statement by his yet uncertain theory that longitude could be established by lunar measurement. He would have to test that theory very thoroughly before he demonstrated it to the learned men of Europe.

Vespucci, the scrupulously honest merchant, certainly preferred the efficient manner in which Portuguese ships were maintained. Spanish captains and crews were inclined to be slack, and their vessels were seldom well handled. No laxity was tolerated on board Portuguese ships, and the standard of navigation was better. Portugal was a poor country by comparison with Spain. Her men had to fish in order to live. They learned their seamanship in small boats, and they also learned to maintain their gear and watch both sea and weather carefully.

From Cape Verde on the coast of West Africa, Vespucci laid his course to the southwest.

> In sixty-four days we arrived at a new land which, for many reasons . . . we observed to be a continent.

This quiet statement announced to the world Vespucci's new and dazzling conviction.

While his three ships lay idly on the glaring surface of the sea, caught in the Equatorial Doldrums, he had spent a great deal of time working out fresh calculations and rechecking his earlier ones. At Cape Verde he had held long conversations with the navigators of Portuguese ships returning from India by the Cape of Good Hope. Everything they told him about India, every estimate they made as to the distances they had sailed, convinced Vespucci once and for all that Ptolemy and Christopher Columbus were wrong. The newly discovered lands on the western side of the Atlantic were *not* an eastward extension of Asia. They comprised an entire new continent, hitherto unsuspected, that lay as a barrier across any direct westerly route to India.

Columbus believed that the circumference of the world at the equator was 18,777 miles. Vespucci himself had calculated it to be more than 22,000 miles. Now he was convinced that the circumference was even larger; he believed the exact figure was 24,852 miles. (He was only 50 miles in error. The actual circumference is 24,902 miles.) His earlier suspicions as to the accuracy of Columbus's claims were proved correct to his complete satisfaction, by the longitude of the Brazilian coast.

Vespucci's ships reached that coast at a latitude about five degrees south of the equator. After taking on fresh water and firewood, he ordered a southerly course to be set.

So began his wonderfully detailed exploration of the east coast of South America. From Cape San Roque, the elbow of Brazil, he sailed southward for a distance that he himself estimated at eight hundred leagues. Allowing for the irregular coastline, the length of the trip down the coast was about 4,000 miles. He reached the bay of Rio de Janeiro in November, 1501. By the middle of January, 1502, he was exploring the great estuary of the Rio de la Plata. At the end of February his men were shivering in the unaccustomed cold of the Bay of St. Julian forty-nine degrees south of the equator. At that point he was only 300 miles north of the still unknown Strait of Magellan, which would have led him westward into the Pacific Ocean.

Vespucci's vigorous imagination was stirred by the wonders of this new country. He knew, however, that Portugal had no claim to much of it. Plotting with his quadrant and astrolabe to find the longitude, he had already ascertained that the Line of Demarcation passed through the coast of Brazil at twenty-five degrees south latitude. His calculation was completely accurate. But what man worthy of the name of explorer could have resisted the temptation to sail still farther south into those unknown seas? Or to chance the discovery of a new ocean? Almost every day revealed fresh marvels.

When Vespucci decided to spend some time among the Indians on the coast near St. Jul-

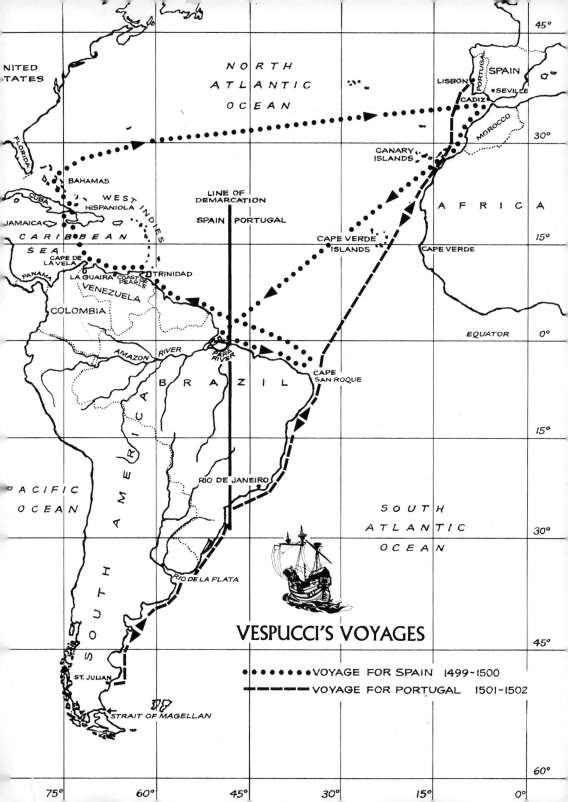

45°

NORTH ATLANTIC OCEAN

UNITED STATES

PORTUGAL SPAIN
LISBON
CADIZ
SEVILLE
MOROCCO

30°

FLORIDA

BAHAMAS

CANARY ISLANDS

AFRICA

CUBA
WEST INDIES
HISPANIOLA

LINE OF DEMARCATION

SPAIN | PORTUGAL

JAMAICA
CARIBBEAN SEA
CAPE DE LA VELA

CAPE VERDE ISLANDS

15°

CAPE VERDE

PANAMA
LA GUAIRA
COAST OF PEARLS
TRINIDAD

VENEZUELA

COLOMBIA

EQUATOR 0°

AMAZON RIVER

PARA RIVER

CAPE SAN ROQUE

BRAZIL

15°

PACIFIC OCEAN

RIO DE JANEIRO

SOUTH ATLANTIC OCEAN

30°

SOUTH AMERICA

RIO DE LA PLATA

VESPUCCI'S VOYAGES

45°

ST. JULIAN

STRAIT OF MAGELLAN

•••••• VOYAGE FOR SPAIN 1499-1500
━━━━━ VOYAGE FOR PORTUGAL 1501-1502

60°

75°   60°   45°   30°   15°   0°

ian, he gave another demonstration of his remarkable courage. The Indians there were the most savage and ferocious he had encountered during his voyages in the New World, but Vespucci was interested in all the details of their daily lives. He wrote:

One can call their cabins truly miraculous houses. For I have seen habitations which are two hundred and twenty paces long and thirty

wide, ingeniously fabricated; and in one of
these houses dwelt five or six hundred persons.

Their food is very good: an endless quan-
tity of fish; a great abundance of sour cherries,
shrimps, oysters, lobsters, crabs, and many other
products of the sea. The meat which they eat
most usually is what one may call human flesh.
When they can get it, they eat other meat, of
animals or birds, but they do not lay hold of
many, for they have no dogs, and the country
is a very thick jungle full of ferocious wild
beasts.

I strove a great deal to understand their conduct and customs. For twenty-seven days I ate and slept among them.

The story of most of that early age of exploration is a miserable record of bloodshed and treachery and of violent sufferings inflicted by Europeans on native races whose only crime, in the eyes of the explorers, was that they knew nothing of Christianity. Vespucci could never have tolerated the cruelties that Spaniards perpetrated wherever they went in the New World. He was fortunate to be able to go exploring in his own quiet, humane, and scientific manner.

Because we went solely to make discoveries and departed from Lisbon with a commission to that effect, and not to seek for any profit, we did not trouble ourselves to search the land or look for any gain. Thus we did not perceive in it anything that would be profitable to anyone. . . . The natives told us of gold and other metals, but I am one of the followers of Saint

Thomas, who are slow to believe. Time will reveal everything.

Vespucci began his northward journey home from fifty degrees south during March, 1502. His ships and men were growing weary and supplies were getting low. During the voyage back to Portugal, he completed the records of his lunar observations. By this time he knew for certain that he indeed had found a scientific method by which longitude could be ascertained. The technique was still difficult and complicated, but at least it was accurate. From now on, explorers who employed the same method would be able to figure out their position accurately.

In the endeavor to ascertain longitude I have lost much sleep, and I have shortened my life by ten years. But I hold it well worth the cost, because if I return in safety from this voyage, I have hopes of winning fame throughout the ages.

Poor Amerigo Vespucci. Through no fault of his, that fame was to be denied him for the next 350 years.

He brought his three ships safely back to Lisbon in June, 1502. From Portugal he wrote another long, descriptive letter to his friend, Lorenzo de' Medici. To the astonished King Emanuel of Portugal and his circle of learned men he announced that the newly discovered countries were part of a new continent.

Geographers were swift to include this almost unbelievable news in their forthcoming maps. Before the end of that year of 1502, such maps were already being printed. Ptolemy was quietly forgotten.

Vespucci himself made his way back to Seville to rest and pick up the threads of his mercantile business. While the whole of Europe discussed his astonishing revelations, he refrained from seeking any publicity or fame. He had spent four years as an explorer, and he had mapped 7,000 miles of coastline—a record no other man could equal. He had discovered the Amazon, Pará, and Plata rivers, and provided the scientific world of those days with accurate geographical information. In addition to these achievements, he had discovered a reliable method of finding longitude. Above all his other accomplishments, he had presented the world with an entire new continent.

It was a tragic misfortune for Vespucci that his friend, Lorenzo de' Medici, died in the year 1503. The letters Vespucci had written to him promptly became almost public property. Certainly they were read and perhaps copied by numerous relatives and friends of those relatives. Such people were more interested in making money for themselves than they were in geographical information about the New World.

No law of copyright existed in those days. An author was utterly unprotected against those who wished to pirate anything he wrote. Amerigo Vespucci's name was famous throughout Europe; the letters he had written would be eagerly read by the public.

Greedy and dishonest writers set to work. The first forgery was entitled *Mundus Novus* (New World). This book came off the printing presses in 1504 with the claim that it contained reprints of Vespucci's letters, written after the Portuguese voyage to Lorenzo de' Medici. The so-called editor prudently remained anonymous. So did the translator. The book was published in Latin, at that time the common language of educated men in Europe. It was printed in Vienna, a great center for dishonest printers.

Mundus Novus was a mixture of truth and fiction. The fellow who prepared it was certainly no seaman. He was not much of a geographer either. The result of his misspent labors was to make Vespucci appear a confused and untidy writer who frequently contradicted himself.

But the book sold in quantities. Only after intelligent and careful men read it did the first doubts regarding Vespucci's reputation begin to grow. Such readers were not aware that *Mundus Novus* was a forgery.

The next book was even more impudent. It appeared a few months after *Mundus Novus* and represented its contents to be four letters written by Vespucci to a certain Piero Soderini of Florence. Soderini, whom history reveals as an unscrupulous and rascally politician, was certainly no friend of the aristocratic Vespucci and Medici families. Vespucci probably knew Soderini, but was not in the habit of writing letters to him.

The *Soderini Letters,* as this latest production became known, was an incomparably worse forgery than *Mundus Novus.* Whoever wrote it in an ungrammatical mixture of Spanish and Italian revealed his own ignorant and unpleasant nature. He made out that Vespucci had taken *four* Atlantic voyages. The first, he claimed, had been in 1497, when Vespucci was actually a merchant in Seville. The last was supposed to have occurred in 1503, when Vespucci was already back in Spain.

Rightly believing that the public liked sensationalism, and that Vespucci had been too scientific and honest for his real letters to enjoy popularity, the forger gave readers what they wanted. Vespucci was portrayed as a boastful adventurer with little regard for the truth, unable to write fluently either in his native Italian or in Spanish.

Vespucci was powerless to prevent the publication of these falsified works or their sale throughout European countries. In Spain, Portugal, and his native Florence, the true facts were known, and so his reputation remained high there. But throughout the rest of Europe, doubts continued to grow as to what Vespucci actually had achieved, and how much of what he said was true. Was he a brilliant explorer? Was he an inaccurate liar? Was it true, as the *Soderini Letters* claimed, that he had reached the coast of South America in 1497, a year before Columbus? Or that he had even made the four voyages he claimed in the book?

Christopher Columbus knew how great a man Vespucci was. They met in 1505 and became friends almost at once. In a letter to his son, Columbus wrote:

> I have talked with Amerigo Vespucci. He has at all times shown a desire to help me, and he is an honorable man. As with many others, fortune has not treated him kindly, and his labors have not been as rewarding as he deserved.

But Vespucci was more fortunate than the aging Columbus. In fact, he always had been luckier than that great old explorer. Unlike Columbus, Vespucci had never had to beg and argue and wait for years before some king gave him the ships he needed. The monarchs came to him and offered him the vessels. He did not have to rely on royal generosity to produce the money he needed to make Atlantic voyages. The funds were always forthcoming. In Spain, Columbus

was regarded as a cantankerous and tiresome man; Vespucci was looked upon with royal favor and affection. He was awarded Spanish nationality by Queen Joanna of Castile:

> In recognition of your fidelity and certain good services you have rendered, and which I expect you will do from henceforward; by this present I make you a native of these my kingdoms of Castile and Leon, with all honors, courtesies, favors, freedoms, exemptions, etc. . . . City of Toro, April 24, 1505.

Martin Waldseemüller was a German professor of geography at a university located near the Franco-German frontiers. He had informed himself of Vespucci's career as an explorer. Unfortunately, perhaps, he relied too much on the *Soderini Letters* for his information. In 1507 he wrote:

> A fourth region (in addition to Europe, Africa, Asia) has been discovered by Americus Vespucius, as may be seen by the attached

charts; in virtue of which I believe it very just that it should be named Amerige. . . after its discoverer, Americus, a man of clever mind; or let it be named America, since both Europa and Asia bear names of feminine form.

Waldseemüller knew all about Columbus's own voyages. He was also aware that Amerigo Vespucci was the first man to announce to Europe that America was a new continent. He believed that the New World should be named after Amerigo and not Columbus, who had failed to identify it correctly.

The name America caught on in the public mind. Waldseemüller's famous map of 1507 used it for the first time. Within a very few years cartographers throughout Europe had also adopted the name.

"I would gladly make one more voyage," Vespucci said to his friends, "in order to discover a sea passage past the new continent to the ocean that leads to Asia. Such a passage must exist, but I know not whether it lies north or south of the equator. I myself would go far south in search of it."

During his exploration of the coast of Brazil, Vespucci had seen how the land gradually sheered away to the west: the direction in which he wanted to go. He was almost certain that no route to the Indies was to be found along the western shores of the Caribbean Sea. The coast of North America was entirely unknown to him.

Vespucci never made that last voyage on which he had set his heart. In 1507, he was fifty-three years old. Shortly after his return to Lisbon in 1502, he married a Spanish woman named Maria Cereso, of whom history has nothing to say. He was in charge of the Spanish Casa de Contratación, which was responsible for the outfitting of all ships making official voyages on behalf of the government of Spain. It was unlikely that he would ever obtain the necessary permission for further exploration. He was too honest, too knowledgeable, and too highly trusted for the Spanish government to grant him an extended leave of absence.

King Ferdinand, who had become regent of Spain, was a clever ruler. He knew how clear-thinking and honest a man he had in Amerigo Vespucci.

Ever since the Western voyages began, Spanish pilots, with the exception of Juan de la Cosa and a few others, had displayed a distressing ignorance of their profession. Vessels supposed to be in mid ocean suddenly crashed onto unexpected shores during the hours of darkness. Islands and ports known to lie in a certain position were often strangely hard to find. Among the cays between Florida and Cuba, galleons mysteriously disappeared never to be heard of

again. Others split their hulls on underwater reefs where some pilot fervently declared there was sufficient depth of water for any ship to sail.

All these misfortunes were costing the Spanish treasury and investors heavy losses. Ferdinand decided that the time had come when pilots must undergo more thorough training. In consultation with old Juan de la Cosa, Pinzon, a veteran navigator, Solis,

who had successfully explored the coast of Honduras, and Amerigo Vespucci, he decided to found a school for pilots. Brushing aside Vespucci's mild protests that he was ambitious to make another voyage, the old monarch named him Pilot Major of Spain. The year was 1508.

The Letter Patent, or official document bestowing this high position on Vespucci, began by setting out the conditions at sea.

The pilots are not sufficiently skillful or acquainted with what they should know in order to be competent to direct and steer the ships that cross the ocean sea to our islands and mainland which we posses in the (West) Indies. Through their incompetence in not knowing how to master and steer, many shipwrecks have occurred. Those who have shipped under their guidance have been exposed to great danger, by which our Lord hath been ill-served as well as our royal exchequer. . . .

After painting this dismal picture of Spanish seafaring conditions, the Letter named the various subjects in which pilots of the future would have to be highly competent.

Without such knowledge no one shall presume to pilot the said ships or receive pay as a pilot, nor may the masters receive them on board, until they have first been examined by you, Amerigo Vespucci, our Chief Pilot.

Whatever the rest of Europe was beginning

to think about Vespucci, his reputation in Spain rose higher than ever. Kings anywhere never have been famous for the high salaries they paid their best officials, but Vespucci was an exception. He was granted a generous salary and various honors that enabled him to live in elegant style.

In addition to his duties as an expert on navigation, Vespucci was given an extra task in which he reveled. All kinds of maps and charts were being used by vessels on transatlantic voyages. Each one differed from the other. Islands and coastlines were inserted in wrong places. Distances were contradictory. Any mention of prevailing winds and currents was often omitted altogether.

Vespucci was given the task of coordinating all these charts. He was expected to produce new sets that were as accurate as possible. Thereafter, every pilot of a Spanish ship would be required to use the Vespucci charts on a voyage to America. Those who failed to do so would be heavily fined.

Vespucci was fifty-four years old when he began his new duties as Pilot Major. He was a handsome and striking figure, who commanded respect wherever he went. His luxuriant hair had turned almost white and reached to his shoulders. His wide-set eyes were as quick and observant as ever. Increasing years had not added cumbersome weight to his muscular body. Throughout Spain and Portugal and Italy he was regarded as one of the greatest men of the age. Astronomers and cartographers, professors and sea captains of those countries eagerly sought his advice.

The pilots who assembled for instruction under him were less in awe of Vespucci's dignified appearance and brilliant record. They were a tough, weather-bronzed, and taciturn body of men. All the story of the

sea was written on their strong faces. In
their time they had faced hurricanes and
mutiny and shipwreck. They had fought
against Indians on the coasts and against
the mountainous waves of the Atlantic
Ocean. Their knowledge of the theory of
navigation was slight, but their practical
experience was enormous. They could ascertain latitude at sea, but they were content
to make ill-judged guesses at longitude.

Often they estimated the speed of a vessel by tossing a piece of wood overboard at the bow and timing how long it took to reach the stern. For time they were content to rely on hourglasses that were often an hour or two in error after a voyage of thirty days. But for all this lack of exact scientific knowledge, a lack that sometimes brought about disaster, the pilots did not want to learn better methods of navigation. They

87

were as conservative in their outlook as seamen the world over always have been. "If longitude can be found by lunar bearings," they argued, "it will not be long before clerks and schoolmasters are taking our employment from us."

Teaching at his School of Pilots was a disappointment for Vespucci. It was impossible to teach men who refused to learn. By this time he knew that he never would make another voyage on his own account. He was too old and the malaria that he had contracted during his first voyage was slowly ruining his health. In any case, Ferdinand of Spain rightly regarded accurate charts and maps as the most important work on which Vespucci could be engaged.

Portuguese authorities shared the Spanish regent's view. Vespucci maps were the best in Europe. His opinion regarding a totally unknown ocean on the western side of America had been completely accepted by Portuguese seamen. In 1511 they were trying to secure copies of his maps to assist them in finding a passage to that ocean. Ferdinand, on the other hand, was determined that no charts prepared by Vespucci should pass into the hands of a rival country. History remains vague as to whether the Portuguese authorities ever succeeded in getting hold of a smuggled chart or two. But one matter is clear: Vespucci's repeated insistence that a passage did exist was what encouraged Magellan to attempt his famous voyage round the world.

Amerigo Vespucci died in Seville on February 22, 1512, at the age of fifty-eight.

He left no great fortune. His integrity had kept him from enriching himself in the Casa de Contratación as many other men would have done. But Spain, a country notoriously ungenerous toward the men who served it best, remembered him and was grateful. His widow was given an adequate state pension.

Seven years after Vespucci's death the Portuguese navigator, Ferdinand Magellan, sailed in quest of a westerly passage to India. In October, 1520, he found the strait that is named after him, and the first voyage around the world was completed by his expedition in September, 1522. Vespucci had been proved right once again.

Almost two hundred years after his death, a marble tablet was placed on the wall of the Vespucci family mansion in Florence in which Amerigo had been born.

Mundus Novus and the *Soderini Letters* continued to ruin Vespucci's name as an explorer for the next 350 years. As late as the 1850's, little more than a hundred years ago, he was still generally regarded as a

TO AMERIGO VESPUCCI

A NOBLE FLORENTINE

WHO BY THE DISCOVERY OF
AMERICA
RENDERED HIS OWN AND HIS
COUNTRY'S NAME ILLUSTRIOUS

THE AMPLIFIER OF THE WORLD

pretentious and untruthful man. His achievements were largely ignored. Pedro Cabral, a Portuguese seamen, explored much of the coast of Brazil in 1500, a year after Vespucci had battled against the adverse currents of its northern coast. Cabral was officially recognized as the discoverer of Brazil. Eminent geographers wrote in scathing terms of Vespucci's modest claims. Yet those same men ignored his discovery of the lunar method of ascertaining longitude that continued to be used by navigators for some 250 years after his death.

There is a Spanish proverb, however, which says: Oil will always rise above water. The truth regarding Vespucci finally began to emerge. Historical writers became more thorough. They grew increasingly wary of accepting popular facts until they had established the truth for themselves. How was it, research students began to ask, that the first editions of the *Soderini Letters* bore all the traces, unmistakable to experts, of being forgeries? Why was it that both books, but particularly the *Soderini Letters,* contained careless mistakes and contradictions that a well-educated writer never would have made? No one could truthfully claim that Vespucci was ill taught or inaccurate. His record as a merchant and as head of the Casa de Contratación proved otherwise. Notes and diaries of his still in existence proved that he was a cultured and extremely intelligent man. Finally, asked the seekers after truth, how did it happen that the *Letters* had been written in a horrid mixture of Italian and Spanish? Could anyone really believe that Vespucci forgot his native Italian language? In any case, his Spanish was equally fluent.

By the 1870's, the first supporters of Vespucci were beginning to express their convictions in print. In the early 1900's, more and more students of history were coming forward to defend him. Eminent American and Italian historians, whose reputations for integrity were above reproach, conclusively proved that both *Mundus Novus* and the *Soderini Letters* were forgeries.

Today it is recognized that the man who gave his name to America was one of the most brilliant explorers and navigators of history. For his discovery of lunar observation alone, his name ranks high in the world of science.

Amerigo Vespucci was undoubtedly the man who revealed the existence of the American continent to the astonished world of Europe.

BIBLIOGRAPHY

Magnaghi, Alberto, *Amerigo Vespucci: Studio Critico.* Rome: Istituto Cristoforo Colombo, 1926.

Markham, Sir Clements R., *The Letters of Amerigo Vespucci and Other Documents Illustrative of His Career.* London: Hakluyt Society, 1894.

Pohl, Frederick J., *Amerigo Vespucci, Pilot Major.* New York: Columbia University Press, 1944.

RONALD SYME spent much of his boyhood in Ireland—his native land—later proceeding to New Zealand, where he spent a few years before going to sea. In 1934 he left the sea to become a professional writer. During World War II Mr. Syme served in the British Merchant Service as a gunner until he was transferred to the British Army Intelligence Corps.

Today Mr. Syme is a well-known author in both England and the United States. He lives in Rarotonga in the Cook Islands of the South Pacific, and he is married to the niece of the paramount chieftain there. His home is a white-walled stone house standing within two hundred yards of a beautiful lagoon and surrounded by palm trees. He uses one large room of his house exclusively as his office. The shelves are lined with books, and Mr. Syme can check almost any historical fact he needs for his writing in his library. He enjoys, as he says, "most of the comforts of civilization without the corresponding disadvantages."